Be.... .....

Your Complete Guide to Ensure You Give Your Betta the Best Life Possible

Anthony Daniels

Table of Contents

Introduction:

Getting a betta fish can be super exciting! However, it can also be stressful if you don't know what you're doing.

Sadly many people who get bettas don't know how to properly take care of them, and the fish usually doesn't live the longest high-quality life that it could. Fortunately, that won't be the case for you any longer.

After reading this book, you'll know all of the ins and outs of taking care of and raising your betta. You'll understand how to properly set up your aquarium, how to feed your betta, how to take care of a sick betta, and much more.

You'll even learn how to breed bettas if you're interested in doing that! Regardless, the first step to being able to properly take care of bettas is having the right information. And by reading this book, you're going to be taking care of that first step. Let's dive right in and get started!

Chapter 1: How Did Bettas Become so Popular as Pets?

The origination of the betta fish or Siamese Fighting Fish started in Southeast Asia. The betta fish was able to adapt and develop into a labyrinth fish (a fish that can breathe in from the air or take in oxygen from its gills) because of the environments the betta found itself in.

Bettas commonly made their homes in rice paddies, drainage ditches, and floodplains. There were commonly floods and droughts in the region, which made the betta adapt into the tough fish we know it as today.

Originally children would collect betta fish and place them together in rice paddies and watch them span. When kept in captivity, bettas will usually fight until death, however in the wild fights will usually only last a few minutes before the losing betta decides to swim away.

Once the popularity of these fish began to take off, the king of Thailand took notice. He started to license and collect betta fish. Then in 1840, the king gave some of his fish to a man who in turn gave them to a physician named Dr. Theodore Cantor.

Dr. Cantor studied and bred them and eventually gave them a name that was already taken by another kind of fish. So he then decided to rename the fish betta splendens, which means beautiful warrior and the name has stuck ever since.

Bettas were first imported to Germany and France during the 1890s, and then they were brought to the U.S. in 1910 by a man named Frank Locke.

It's also interesting to note that Americans will sometimes mispronounce the fish's name by calling it "bay-tuh." It's actually believed that this species of fish was named after the ancient Bettah warrior tribe, which was pronounced "bet-tah." Therefore, you should pronounce the word as "bet-tah" and not "bay-tuh."

And if you've been calling it the wrong thing you're entire life you're not the only one! I grew up most of my whole life calling it "bay-tuh," and I still call it that sometimes out of habit. Regardless of how you've been pronouncing it, it's still important and interesting to think about where the name betta originally came from.

Why Get a Betta as a Pet?

So really the betta only started becoming popular as a pet during the late 19th century and the early 20th century. Of course, it's easy to see why keeping a betta as a pet became so popular so quickly. They have beautiful and bright colors, lush fins, and they're the easiest freshwater fish to take care of—perfect for beginners.

The harsh and unpredictable environments these bettas' ancestors grew up in allowed them to adapt and be able to better withstand harsher conditions. Not that you should get sloppy with the care of your betta—we want it to have the best quality of life possible!

And assuming that you follow the instructions in this book for how to properly take care of your betta, your betta should have no problem living a full life of around 3-5 years, which is the average lifespan of a betta fish.

There are a lot of myths that surround bettas, and many of them probably started because of the "toughness" of bettas. People figure that if their ancestors could survive in the harsh environmental conditions of Southeast Asia, then surely it's ok if they live in a small tank or have dirty water.

False! Just because a betta could survive in harsh conditions, it doesn't follow that it should have to live in harsh conditions. Not to worry though, this book will dispel some of the most common myths about bettas, and it'll give you the proper guidance for taking care of them.

Sadly many pet store workers don't know the info contained in this book. They only know what they've been told by their coworkers, which is probably limited and false information to begin with. Not only that, but you have to consider that these stores are trying to make a profit. They might try to sell you things that might not be the best for your betta, or sell you things that you don't really need.

I'll tell you exactly what you do need and do not need for your aquarium. Some of it might surprise you, and it might go against what you've been told about bettas before, but remember there are a lot of myths out there surrounding bettas.

You need to have the right information in order to properly care for your betta. Sadly, most don't have the right information when it comes to taking care of betta fish, but you fortunately do. So with that out of the way, it's time for you to learn everything you'll need to properly set up your tank and how to do it.

Chapter 2: How to Properly Set Up Your Aquarium

Getting a new betta fish is very exciting, and it can be tempting to want to immediately take a bowl, fill it up with water, and put your new fish in it. If this is what you want to do, then you need to take a deep breath and slow down! The first thing you must consider before you even buy your betta is what size aquarium you want to buy.

It's a common myth that bettas don't need a lot of space, or that they prefer to be in smaller enclosures. That certainly isn't the case!

I think this misconception comes about because we see bettas in small cups at the pet store, and we also see many betta aquariums are less than a gallon in size! This doesn't mean that we should put our betta fish in a quarter gallon or half-gallon sized tank.

Sure you might know someone who had his or her betta do just fine in a small enclosure, but you have to realize that's the exception, not the rule. You must not confuse simply surviving with optimal living conditions.

Briefly imagine for a second a dog that's chained up. He won't be able to move very much, but he's still brought food and water to keep him alive.

So is the dog living? Yes, the dog is certainly still alive. However, is the dog living an optimal quality of life?

Certainly not! What does it take for a dog to be happy? It needs to be able to run around freely and have someone to play with and love him. Simply giving the dog food and water isn't enough.

The same applies to betta fish. Sure a betta's needs are going to differ from a dog's, but you get the idea.

Therefore, the minimum tank size you should get for your betta is 2.5 gallons. Anything less than that isn't going to give it an optimal amount of space to move around.

So avoid any bowls or vases. Some will buy a vase and put a betta in there with a plant.

This is a big mistake! The main idea behind this is that the betta will be able to feed out of the nutrients from the plant, and then the plant will be able to absorb and use the waste from the fish as food.

In theory, this sounds like a good idea, but it isn't healthy for your betta fish. The reason is that bettas are carnivores, not herbivores.

Carnivores eat meaty foods in their diet, whereas herbivores only eat plants. Bettas, therefore, need a good source of protein in their diet, and the plant will not provide this.

I'll discuss more about how and what to feed your betta in another chapter, but for now, know that putting your betta in a vase with a plant isn't a good idea!

Not only that, but getting a larger tank is actually going to be easier to clean and maintain. The reason being is that harmful toxins such as ammonia will build up faster in a smaller tank size, and thus will require water changes more often.

You'll also want to make sure that you get a tank with a lid on it. You don't want the top of the aquarium to be exposed!

The reason for this is that bettas can sometimes jump out of the tank, and they'll unfortunately die if you're not there to save him in time! After the aquarium is picked out, the next thing you'll want to get is a heater.

The reason for this is because bettas are tropical fish. This means that they like having warmer water temperatures of 78 degrees Fahrenheit or above.

Anything less than that could stress your betta out, or cause it to go into shock. Maintaining an optimal temperature in your aquarium would be really hard to do without a heater. A heater in an aquarium works much the same way that the air conditioner in your house does.

When the heater in the tank detects that the temperature is less than 78 degrees, it'll come on and stay on until the tank's temperature comes up to 78 degrees. Some heaters are automatically preset to 78 degrees and others will allow you to adjust the temperature.

It really depends on what you want to buy because either option will work great. The main thing though is that you'll want to get a heater!

I'm sure some people will try to tell you that you don't need a heater for your betta, but remember we're talking about optimal conditions here! I got my first betta when I was 10 years old and he died on Christmas morning because a cold front came in, and I didn't know you needed a heater.

Yes it was sad, but at least I now know that deaths like this can be prevented if you get the necessary equipment! The next thing you'll want to consider getting is a filter.

The necessity of getting a filter for a betta is up for debate among fish enthusiasts. Some say that a filter isn't necessary because bettas are labyrinth fish.

This means that bettas can receive oxygen from the air from the top of your tank. Bettas can also receive oxygen from the water as well. Therefore some will conclude that a filter isn't necessary because the oxygenation system that the filter would be providing wouldn't be necessary.

Yet, there are others who say that you should get a filter for your betta. The other thing that a filtration system will do is help to clean up fish waste and harmful toxins such as ammonia and other nitrates.

And since the filter will be cleaning the water, it'll also mean that you can do less water changes. Ultimately the choice is up to you, but if it were me, I would ease on the side of caution and get a filter.

If you do decide to get a water filter, you'll want to make sure you get one that's appropriate for your tank size. For example, if you have a 5 gallon tank, and you buy a filter that's meant for a 30 gallon tank, then the flow that filter creates is going to be too strong for your betta.

Betta's are weak swimmers, they have long and lush fins that slow them down when swimming. Having a filter that's too strong will create a current in your tank that your betta will have a difficult time being able to swim through if anything.

Bettas prefer calmer water. That's why you'll want to get a filter with which you can adjust the intensity of, or buy a filter that naturally has a low flow to begin with. After the filter, the next thing you'll want to consider is substrate.

Substrate is simply what will go along the bottom of your tank. Some people like the look of not having any substrate at all, but this is a big mistake.

Beneficial bacteria, which will help to "eat up" and take care of some of the harmful toxins in your tank accumulate in your substrate. If you don't have any substrate, then you'll be missing out on a good amount of beneficial bacteria to help eliminate toxins.

In terms of which substrate you can use, you have two options of gravel or sand. If you're a beginner, using gravel is going to be much easier to deal with.

When you're first setting up your tank, it's not going to cloud it up. It's also much easier to clean, and you're going to have an easier time maintaining a proper pH level in your tank.

Sand contains calcium carbonate, which can raise the pH level in your tank. Bettas prefer to have a pH range of 6.5 to 8.0.

The measure of pH in your tank essentially measures how acidic or basic the water in your tank is. The pH ranges from 0-14. The closer the pH is to 0 the more acidic the water is. The closer the pH is to 14, the more basic the water is.

To get a little technical, pH measures the amount of free hydrogen and hydroxyl ions in the water. Ultimately the choice of using sand or gravel is up to you, however if you're a beginner when it comes to taking care of fish, starting off with gravel is going to be easier to handle.

And if you're not sure of what the pH level in your tank is, you can take a sample of your tank water to a local pet store. Most pet stores have free water testing, which will allow you to know your pH, ammonia, and nitrate levels among other things.

And if you don't mind investing a little bit of money, you can buy a water testing kit, and test the pH yourself! Finally, you want to add decorations to your tank.

Some people like the look of a bare tank, but you'll want to avoid this when it comes to bettas. Bettas like to have places to hide behind or swim under to feel safe.

This helps to mimic their natural environment, which will make them happier and less stressed. Of course, you can buy whatever type of decorations you want, but you'll want to consider what type of specific plant decorations you'll get.

The reason for this is because you can, of course, go with real or fake plants. If you're a beginner and you haven't taken care of fish before, I'd recommend going with fake plants.

This is going to give you one less thing to have to worry about, and it'll allow you to focus your attention solely on taking care of the fish. If you buy live plants, then you'll have to worry about getting the right lighting for the plants, as well as potentially having to buy other supplements to help feed the plants as well.

For beginners, it's certainly easier to buy fake plants so you won't have to worry about it. Of course, when it comes to buying fake plants, you can buy plastic or silk plants.

Preferably go with the silk plants here. The reason for this is because the plastic plants can be a little bit rougher around the edges.

When your betta swims by these plants, the edges of its fins might get torn up over time. It's simply a safer bet to go with silk plants for the health of your betta's fins.

Now that you have the decorations picked out, the last thing you'll need to consider is the water that you'll be using.

Filling up your tank with tap water from your faucet isn't a good idea. Tap water contains many harmful chemicals that'll potentially kill your betta.

If you're going to use tap water, make sure that you buy a water conditioner from the pet store or online. The water conditioner will get rid of the harmful chemicals (such as chlorine) contained in the water, which will then make it safe for the fish.

The cool thing is that water conditioner isn't that expensive, and you don't have to use much of it to make the tap water safe. Alternatively, you could also use spring water that you buy from the store.

This might get to be a little inconvenient if you don't have some handy whenever you do water changes, but it'll work just as good as the water conditioner.

Now you're just about ready to go! Everything should be set up perfectly in your tank to your liking. Your betta will have everything that it needs to live a happy high-quality life.

At this point, you might be tempted to immediately put your betta in the tank. However, I would urge you to be a little patient.

Once you get your tank set up, it's ideal to wait for 24 hours before you put your betta in the tank. This will give the temperature time to stabilize so it won't fluctuate as much and potentially cause your betta to go into shock.

Once you've waited 24 hours with the tank fully set up and the heater running, you'll want to do one last thing. You'll want to float the betta in the cup you bought it in, on the surface of the tank.

The reason for this is because the temperature inside of the betta's cup might be different from the temperature inside the tank. If you don't float your fish, and you instead put it straight in the tank, this might cause the fish to go into shock, causing it to die.

By floating your fish in the cup you bought it in on the surface of the tank, you'll allow any temperature differences between the two to equalize. I know it can be tempting to immediately put the fish in the tank, but waiting for a day is optimal.

If you have to leave your betta in the cup you bought it in for another 24 hours, then do so. Your betta will be fine because if you didn't buy it, it would still be sitting in that same cup in the pet store anyways!

Chapter 3: How to Feed Your Betta

As I mentioned in the previous chapter, bettas are carnivores. They need a good source of protein in their diet. When it comes to feeding your betta, you have some different options:

Flakes: you can certainly feed your betta flakes if you like. You'll want to make sure that you buy flakes that are made for fish that are carnivores.

Many tropical fish are omnivores, meaning that they eat a diet consisting of meat and plants. Of course, some bettas will straight up not eat flakes, and if this is the case for your betta, then you'll need to try something else.

Pellets: buying pellets that are specifically made for bettas is probably the best way to go. These pellets will contain the right amount of nutrition that your betta needs, it'll be the correct size, and it won't sink too fast.

Other pellet foods are too big and your betta will struggle to consume them. Some pellets will sink too fast, and remember your betta is a slower swimmer, which will make it difficult to catch the sinking pellets.

Live food: you can also feed your betta live food such as live bloodworms and brine shrimp. Your betta will certainly love it!

The only downside with it is that it can be inconvenient to feed your betta live food, and it can get to be quite expensive.

But you can certainly feed your betta live food as a treat from time to time.

Frozen food: instead of buying bloodworms and brine shrimp live, you can buy them frozen. This will allow you to buy them in bulk and they'll stay good for a long time.

However, similar to live food, buying your betta frozen food can get to be pretty expensive if it's your betta's main food source. If it does get to be too expensive, then you can use frozen food as a treat.

Freeze-dried food: this is another way you can feed your betta to help introduce him to foods like brine shrimp or bloodworms. However, if you're going to feed your pet the freeze-dried version, it's best to offer it as a treat.

Freeze-dried foods have much of their moisture taken away, and they contain other added fillers to make them last longer. The good news is that they're cheap, and can be stored for a relatively long period of time.

How Often Should You Feed Your Betta?

The thing you must first consider is how small betta's stomachs are. A betta's stomach is approximately the size of its eyeball. So as you can imagine, it doesn't take very much food to fill up a betta.

If you're feeding your betta fish pellets for example, you should only feed your betta approximately 3 pellets. In terms of how often you should feed them, this can vary.

Feeding your betta once a day works great because you still won't be overfeeding your betta, and it makes it easier to keep a consistent feeding schedule.

You can also feed your betta 3 pellets every other day if you like as well. It really is up to you.

Bettas can actually go up to two weeks before starving to death. So not feeding them one day won't hurt them.

Of course, this doesn't mean that you should only feed them once every two weeks, this fact is just meant to put into perspective how little food bettas need.

Humans can go awhile without food as well, but that doesn't mean we enjoy it! Another benefit to bettas is that you won't have to worry about feeding them over the weekend if you have a pet betta at the office or something like that.

If this is the case for you, then feeding your betta 5 days of the week will work perfectly fine. If you decide to feed your betta fish a treat, such as freeze-dried bloodworms for example, then you'll want to forego what you normally feed them.

For example, if you usually feed your betta 3 pellets, then instead you'll feed your betta 3 bloodworms. It's important that you don't overfeed your betta because this can cause them to become sick.

Additionally, if your betta doesn't eat all of the food, then the leftovers can start to build up bacteria and harmful toxins over time. That's why it's a good idea to scoop out any uneaten food after your betta is done eating.

Overall, feeding your betta is fairly simple, and by not overfeeding your fish, you'll help to keep him healthy, and it'll make it easier to keep the tank clean!

Chapter 4: Tips You Should Know When Cleaning Your Betta's Tank

Every now and again, there will come a time when you'll need to clean your betta's aquarium. However, there are many things people commonly do that are completely wrong and harmful to their betta when they clean out the tank.

I myself was guilty of some of these back in the day. Let's get started...

Tip #1: Rinse Your Hands

You'll want to make sure that you thoroughly rinse your hands before you start to clean your betta's tank. The key is to only use water though and not soap.

Soap residue is harmful to your betta so it's best to avoid it all together. This will help to prevent you accidentally introducing any harmful bacteria into your tank.

Tip #2: Don't Change Out All of the Water

When I was a kid I had a 10-gallon fish tank. I would mistakenly overfeed my fish, which would then cause the water to become really murky quite quickly.

When my dad and I would go to clean the tank, we would take all of the fish out and put them in a separate bucket.

Then we would dump all of the old water out, clean the gravel, and then proceed to fill up the tank with fresh new water. A lot of the times though my fish would end up dying within the next day or two and sadly I never understood why.

Now I know that it could've been for a couple of different reasons...

The first would be a big fluctuation in temperature. When you're adding that much new water to a tank, it's unlikely going to be the same temperature as your old water.

And as I mentioned earlier, a big fluctuation in temperature can cause your fish to go into shock and die. The other thing that was happening was that by cleaning out all of the old water and gravel we were destroying any of the beneficial bacteria that had built up over time.

This made it much easier for toxins to build up and harm the fish. This is why you'll want to do partial water changes.

It's not necessary to change out 100% of the water each and every time you need to clean your tank. Of course, how often you'll need to clean your tank will depend on a couple of things like whether or not you're using a filter in your tank.

A good general rule of thumb is to clean out 10-15% of your tank's water every 1-2 weeks. Betta's don't create too much waste, and if it's the only fish in your tank you'll likely be able to go a good two weeks before you need to do a water change.

How you will remove the water from your tank will really depend on the size of the tank. If you're dealing with a smaller tank, then you can simply use something like a cup to remove the necessary amount of water.

On the other hand, if you're dealing with a larger tank, something like 10 gallons or bigger, then you may want to consider investing in a siphoning hose.

This will allow you to quickly and easily drain the necessary amount of water from your tank into a separate bucket. It'll also allow you to clean up any waste that has accumulated in the gravel.

Once you have removed the old water, you can then add in the new water. Of course, make sure that you don't add tap water to your betta's tank!

The best thing to do is to add the tap water to a separate bucket and then add the water conditioner to the bucket before adding it to the tank. And of course, if you're using spring water, then you can simply just add it straight to the tank.

Tip #3: Keep the Betta in the Tank

You might think that you'll need to remove your betta from the tank before you clean it, but this isn't necessary at all. In fact, removing the betta could cause it to go into shock if you use new water that wasn't originally from the tank.

There could also be a mishap when transferring the fish (yes this has happened to me before), or your betta could even jump out of the temporary bowl you put it in!

It's best to simply leave the fish in the tank and simply avoid scooping him up with a cup or getting close to him with the siphoning hose. However, if you feel more comfortable doing water changes with your betta in a separate tank, then you can certainly do so.

Make sure that you use current water from the tank your betta is in, and also make sure the top of the bowl is covered in a way that still allows him to breathe but not be able to jump out!

Tip #4: Keep Decorations in the Tank

You won't need to clean off your decorations every time you do a water change in your fish tank. The main reason for this is because there's not much of a point to do so.

Yes over time, your decorations and plants can build algae on them, and if you start to notice this happening, then it would be a good time to take them out and clean them. When you do clean your decorations, make sure that you only use water and a clean brush (such as a new tooth brush).

You'll want to avoid using soap as this can contaminate your tank. You might want to move your decorations around to make it easier to clean the gravel if you're using a siphoning hose.

Aside from that tough, you really don't need to worry about cleaning your decorations.

Tip #5: Use an Algae Sponge to Clean the Walls of the Tank

You might notice algae start to build up on the sides of the tank walls. If you start to notice this, you can simply clean it up using an algae sponge.

You'll want to use something that's specifically made for fish tanks to ensure the material it's made of won't scratch the glass of your tank.

Of course, you can use a regular algae sponge, which will require you to dip your hand and arm in the tank, or you can use a magnetic algae sponge. This two piece magnet contains a sponge that's placed on the inside of the tank and a handle that's placed on the outside of the tank that then connects to the piece inside the aquarium.

This'll allow you to easily clean the algae inside the tank from the outside so you won't have to worry about getting your arm wet. Pretty nice if you ask me!

That's really all there is to cleaning your betta's tank. They don't create a lot of waste to begin with, and a filter will help a lot with maintaining the tank in the first place if you choose to use one.

Chapter 5: Signs Your Betta May Be Sick and How to Take Care of It

Even if you do everything right, your betta may still get sick. This can be very concerning, however if you know what to look for and how to treat it, you'll be able to quickly fix the problem before it gets out of hand.

Here are some of the signs you'll need to look out for to determine if your betta is feeling sick:

Not as active: if you notice the activity levels of your betta go down, then this could be a sign that something is up. If your betta starts to hang out at the bottom of the tank more often than usual, then this could be a sign that your temperature might not be optimal.

You can use a thermometer made for aquariums to make sure you're at the correct range for bettas, which would be between 78-82 degrees Fahrenheit.

Not interested in food: if your betta is eating normally and then it stops eating or showing interest in food, then your betta might be sick. It might also just not like the food you're feeding it, so vary your betta's diet and see if that does the trick.

If it doesn't, then it's quite possible that something is wrong with your betta.

Fin rot: your betta's fins should look full and lush. If you start to notice your betta's fins rotting away or developing rips or holes, then something is probably wrong with your fish.

Fin rot will usually occur whenever your betta is stressed. It could be stressed for any number of reasons, but the first thing you must do is recognize it.

Fins clamped to its body: another sign that your betta is stressed out is that its fins are clamped to its sides. Your betta's fins should be fanned out and not clamped down to the side of its body.

Small white specks across your betta's body: if you notice white speckled dots across your betta's body, then this could be a symptom of a certain parasite called Ich.

Rubbing against the side of the tank: another sign that your betta may be sick is if he regularly starts to rub his body up against the side of the tank or against decorations that you have in your tank.

Odd traits: if your betta starts to display odd traits such as raised scales, bulging eyes, or if he's unable to open and close his gills, then something might be wrong with your betta.

Abnormal breathing: yes bettas are labyrinth fish meaning that they can get oxygen from the air or from the water in the tank. However, if you notice your betta is always at the top of the tank trying to get air, then something might be wrong.

Loss of color: your betta's colors should be bright and vibrant. That's probably one of the reasons you wanted a betta fish in the first place! If you start to notice the colors of your betta get dull, then your fish could be sick.

Identifying and Treating Your Betta

Ultimately only a professional such as a licensed veterinarian can diagnose your betta with a certain disease. However, some betta illnesses are very common and they can be treated right from your own home.

Treating Fin Rot: fin rot is fairly common among bettas and its symptoms are clamped fins or deteriorating fins. The good news is that this can be fixed and reversed depending on how quickly you notice and fix it.

The fins will grow back over time, however they might not be as lush as they were to begin with. Regardless, the first thing you need to do is make sure that you have a clean tank.

Make sure that you're doing regular water changes and keeping the water clean. This will help your betta recover from the fin rot, and it'll help prevent it from happening again in the future.

During the time when your fish has fin rot it would be ok to do daily water changes of around 20-30%. You want the water to be as clean as possible to help your betta recover.

Aside from that, you'll want to get some fish medicine such as Melafix, Maracyn, or Tetracyclin. You can also add some aquarium rock salt to your betta's tank as well to help treat fin rot.

This will help with the functioning of your fish's gills and help maintain your betta's natural slime coat. Of course, make sure that you're using salt that's actually made for aquariums and not regular table salt!

Treating Ich: Ich can be a very scary thing, and I've even lost some fish to it myself. You must catch Ich quickly and know how to treat it to ensure the best chance of survival.

A common symptom of Ich is small white dots scattered across your betta's body. One good way to help prevent Ich in the first place is to use aquarium rock salt.

Since the salt will regenerate and maintain your betta's slime coat, it'll be much harder for it to get infected with Ich to begin with. Also thoroughly check any betta fish before you buy it and look to see if it has any white spots on its body.

Finally, if you're going to buy live plants for your tank, check to make sure no fish are housed in the same tank as the plants. If they are, then there's a possibility that the plants may be infected with the disease from one of the fish it's being housed with.

However, if your betta already has Ich you probably don't care too much about how to prevent it right now. So how can you treat Ich?

One option you have is raising the temperature of your tank. The right amount of heat can quickly kill off the parasite.

Ideally, you'll want to increase the temperature of your tank to around 85-86 degrees Fahrenheit. At 85 degrees Fahrenheit, Ich will no longer infect your fish.

And at 86 degrees Fahrenheit, Ich will stop being able to reproduce. You'll want to do this slowly and steadily so your betta can adapt to the temperature change.

If you go straight from 78 degrees to 86 degrees Fahrenheit for example, then your betta is likely to get overheated and die. Therefore gradually change the temperature 1-2 degrees Fahrenheit every couple of hours to give your fish time to adapt.

Of course, this may not work for you if you have a heater that's preset to 78 degrees and can't be changed. I also wouldn't recommend doing this if you have a tank that's 5 gallons or smaller.

Smaller tanks can overheat rather quickly and kill your fish. However, if you can't increase the temperature of your tank, don't fret. There are other things you can do to treat the issue.

As with fin rot, you'll want to make sure that you do daily water changes of around 20-30% to fully replace the old water with fresh clean water. You'll also want to treat your tank with aquarium rock salt.

You'll want to use approximately 1 teaspoon of salt per gallon of water. You'll want to add this salt to the fresh water that you'll be adding to the tank when you do your water changes and not the old water that you'll be replacing.

If you don't want to use aquarium salt, you can use medicine specifically designed to take care of Ich such as Ich Attack. It's not recommended to use both aquarium rock salt and Ich medicine because the combination of these two things can restrict oxygen levels in your tank.

If you do decide to use the Ich medicine simply follow the instructions on the bottle according to your tank size.

Treating Popeye: popeye is fairly easy to recognize—if one or both of your betta's eyes appear to be bulging out from its body, then it probably has popeye. Popeye can be a sign of something far more serious such as tuberculosis, which sadly isn't treatable.

However, most of the times popeye occurs due to dirty tank water, and if this is the case then it can be fixed. You'll want to do daily water changes of around 20-30% until all of the old water in your tank is replaced with fresh clean water.

You'll also want to use an antibacterial treatment for your betta as well such as Ampicillin. Even after the symptoms of popeye have disappeared, you'll still want to perform a water change of around 10-20% every 2-3 days and continue treating your tank with the medication for up to a week after the symptoms have disappeared.

Treating Fungal Infections: if you notice that your betta's colors seem duller than usual or that your betta isn't as active as it usually is, then it might have a fungal infection. You betta might also have what appear to be white cotton patches on its body.

Again the main thing you'll want to do is perform daily water changes of 20-30% until all of the old water is replaced (are you starting to notice a theme here?). Aside from that, you'll also want to treat the fungal infection with medication such as Fungus Cure.

Swim Bladder Disorder: a betta that can't swim horizontally or a betta that will float on one side characterizes swim bladder disorder. Your fish might even remain at the bottom of the tank because swimming is too difficult.

Swim bladder disorder usually occurs from overfeeding your betta fish. The cool thing about swim bladder is that your betta can recover from this on its own.

The main thing you'll want to do is pay attention to how much you're feeding it. Remember bettas have small stomachs that are about the size of their eyeball. You'll only want to feed your betta 3 pellets every day or every other day to ensure that you don't overfeed it.

How to Prevent Disease and Illness in the First Place

The best thing you can do for your betta is to take the precautionary measures to prevent a disease or illness from happening in the first place. Yes even if you're doing everything right, sometimes your fish might get sick.

Even with that being the case, a lot of these diseases can be prevented. A common theme that you might've noticed in treating these illnesses was regular water changes.

Having a dirty tank makes your fish much more susceptible to contracting an illness. That's why it's so important to do regular water changes on your aquarium every couple of weeks.

It also might be a good idea to get a filter for your tank because the filter will help to keep the tank clean as well. Aside from regular water changes, you can also add aquarium rock salt to your tank to help prevent diseases.

To do this, simply add ½ teaspoon of aquarium rock salt to your tank for every gallon. You don't need to add the salt every day for example, you can add it in every time you do a regular water change (so every couple of weeks for example).

Chapter 6: How to Teach Your Betta Fish Cool Tricks

Did you know that you could actually teach your betta fish how to do neat tricks like jump, come, flare, and swim through a hoop? Seriously bettas aren't just some boring fish that you watch swim around—you can teach them how to do some pretty cool things.

Here's how you can make your betta the coolest one on the block:

Step #1: Make Sure Your Betta is Healthy

If you notice signs of illness with your betta such as rotting fins or your betta not being as active as it usually is, then you'll want to make sure you get him healthy first.

Think about it. When you're sick, do you feel like doing much of anything?

My guess is probably not, and the same goes for your betta! You can refer to the earlier chapter about spotting and treating illnesses your betta might have. Once you've made sure your betta is healthy, it's time to move onto the next step.

Step #2: Become Accumulated with Your Betta

You'll want to get to know your betta fairly well before you start trying to teach it tricks. If you try to teach your betta how to flare on command on the first day you have it, then you might not be too successful.

The reason for this is because betta fish will actually begin to recognize you after a while. Your betta will start to become more attached to you the more time you spend around its tank.

It might even start swimming around vigorously once it sees you start to approach the tank. So make sure that you spend a good amount of time getting to know your betta for at least a week or so before you start trying to teach it tricks.

Step #3: Have Something to Reward Your Betta With

Animals and humans work on the pain/pleasure principle. We'll do something to get a reward or to avoid pain.

So for example, if a teenager misses his or her curfew and gets grounded, he'll learn to get home on time so he can avoid that pain of being grounded.

For your betta fish there's not much you can really do to punish it (not that you should be doing that anyway), so instead it's much better and productive to focus on using positive rewards for your fish.

And the best thing to reward your betta with is food. Now you have to be careful with this because you can overfeed your betta rather quickly.

So if you're going to start training your betta to learn new tricks, it's best to use the food it would normally be eating as a reward instead of feeding it extra food.

And of course, before you start interacting with your betta and feeding it food, make sure that you rinse off your hands without soap. Soap can be toxic to fish.

Step #4: Get Your Betta to Notice You

The first thing you need to do is start training your betta to start following your finger. To do this put a food pellet under your nail or get the edge of your finger wet so the piece of food will stick to your finger better.

You can also use some other piece of food such as part of a bloodworm. After you have the piece of food on your hand, you'll want to get your betta's attention.

You can get him to notice you by waving your finger in front of the glass or by softly tapping the glass of the tank. Once you have your betta's attention, you can start teaching it different tricks.

Step #5: Teaching Your Betta to Follow Your Finger

The first trick you can teach your betta is how to follow your finger. The first thing you'll want to do is make sure that you have your betta's attention.

Once you do, you can start to move your finger from one side of the tank to the other. If your betta starts to follow your finger, immediately reward your fish with a piece of food.

After that, you can move your finger vertically, and if your betta follows you, reward him. You can practice training your betta with this trick for 3-5 minutes 2-3 times per week.

Once your betta gets really good at following your finger, teaching him other tricks will be a lot easier.

Step #6: Teaching Your Betta How to Flare

Watching your betta flare its fins out is really cool. I remember as a kid one of my favorite things was to get a mirror and watch my betta flare out its fins.

Of course, you don't want to do this too often because it'll stress your fish out. Regardless, the easiest way to start training your betta to flare is to get a mirror and put it in front of your betta.

Then once your betta flares, immediately put a pen next to the mirror. Also, make sure that you're consistent about the color of the pen you're using so your betta can easily recognize it every time.

Then after a couple times of placing the pen next to the mirror when the betta flares, you can move to the next step. The next step would be removing the mirror once it causes your betta to flare and replace it with the pen instead of putting the pen beside the mirror.

Then once your betta remains flaring at the pen, give it a treat. Keep repeating this until your betta gets to the point where you only have to show it the pen in order to get it to flare.

Step #7: Teach Your Betta to Swim Through a Hoop

To get your betta to learn how to swim through a hoop, the first thing you need to do is get a pipe cleaner and bend part of it to make a circle that's approximately 2 inches in diameter. Then use the other end of the pipe cleaner to make a hook, and hang the pipe cleaner on the edge of your tank.

After that, you're going to want to put a piece of food on your finger. Then once you have your betta's attention, move your finger along the tank, guiding your betta through the hoop.

If your betta goes through the hoop, reward it with a piece of food. After your betta gets good at this, you can start to decrease the size of the hoop, still rewarding your betta each time it successfully swims through the hoop.

Of course, make sure that the hoop is still big enough for your betta to be able to swim through it. Then you can start to move the hoop farther away from the side of the tank.

Keep working with your betta until it gets to the point where it'll swim through the hoop whenever you place the pipe down in the middle of the tank.

Step #8: Teach Your Betta How to Jump

Teaching your betta how to jump is probably one of the easier tricks for your betta to learn how to do. This is because it's a betta's natural instinct to want to jump.

This is why you'll want to make sure you normally have a hood on your tank! To teach your betta how to jump, you'll want to put a piece of food on your finger and get your betta's attention.

Then place your finger above the surface of the water, but not so high up to where your betta won't be able to reach the food. Your betta should then jump up to eat the food off your finger.

Once your betta gets comfortable with this, you can extend the distance of your finger slightly. You don't want to overstrain your fish so be wise about it.

And that's how you can teach your betta cool different tricks! It might take a while for your betta to get the hang of some of these things, so the best thing you can do is be patient.

Keep practicing until your betta gets the hang of it. The first and most basic thing you'll need to teach your betta is how to follow your finger.

After that, you can teach it any trick you like in any order, it really is up to you. Teaching it how to jump is probably the easiest trick for it to learn so that would be a good place to start.

Chapter 7: How to Breed Betta Fish

You may be interested in doing more than just owning a betta fish. You might want to breed bettas as well. Of course, I must warn you that this isn't going to be cheap or easy necessarily.

However, I still want to provide you with the basics of what to do in case you're interested in breeding bettas.

Step #1: Know What You're Getting Yourself Into

The idea of breeding bettas certainly sounds cool, but you really need to know exactly what it is that you're getting yourself into. It's not as simple as putting a male and female betta together in the same tank and waiting.

It's a very time-consuming and expensive process. I also wouldn't recommend doing it as a way of making money, I personally don't believe it's worth all of the hassle and that there are far easier ways to make money.

Not only that, but you also have to consider what type of betta's you want to breed and what you're going to do with all of the fry.

Some bettas will lay upwards of 500 eggs! While this is rare, it can still happen, but somewhere in the range of 100 is more common.

100 eggs are still quite a lot, and you'll need to know what to do with all of these new little hatchlings. These are all things that you need to think about before trying to breed bettas.

Step #2: Set Up Your Permanent Tanks for the Bettas

Once you know exactly what it is that you're getting yourself into, you'll then need to set up the tanks for the bettas that you're going to be breeding. You'll want to have a tank set up with everything that was mentioned in the previous chapter.

Then you'll want to get a clear divider for your tank, or you can have two separate tanks side by side. The reason for this is because initially the male and female bettas will be separated, but they still need to be able to see and interact with each other.

Step #3: Get the Correct Breeding Pair

You might think breeding bettas is as simple as going to the pet shop, picking out a male and female betta that you like, putting them together, and boom you've got yourself some new fry. The betta's you get matter a great deal.

If you get your bettas at a pet shop, you won't know how old the bettas are and you won't know much about their genetic history.

Why does this matter? First of all, you'll want to know the bettas' age because bettas breed best when they're around the ages of 4-12 months old.

Not only that, but it's best to let your betta settle into its new environment for about a month before you try to start breeding with it. So if you get a betta that's already 12 months old, it could be too late for it to start breeding.

You have to understand that there's no real way of knowing how long the betta has been sitting at the pet store for. And trying to take shortcuts at this point is only going to cause you more pain and frustration in the long run.

You must also consider the genetics of the betta. If the betta has a poor genetic history, then the fry might get sick or not turn out the way you wanted them to.

That's why the best option is to get your bettas from a reputable breeder. The breeder will be able to tell you the exact age of the fish and give you a good history of the bettas you might potentially buy so that you know more of what to expect.

The other thing you must think about is getting a male betta that your female will like. In the betta kingdom, the females are the picky sex, and in the wild they'll watch males fight and determine which of them are worthy to mate with.

We're not going to have males fight against each other, so we'll have to use other signs that might indicate a strong male to the potential female suitor.

Therefore, when picking out a male betta, you'll want to pay attention to his activity levels. Is he lethargic or active?

You'll want to choose a male betta that's active. The next thing you want to look for is the coloration of the betta.

Are his colors bright and vibrant or dull? Try to pick out a betta that has bright and bold colors.

Finally, pay attention to the betta's fins. Do they look full and healthy? Do they have any holes or rips in them?

Does the betta show any other signs of illness or disease? These are all signs that you'll want to look out for when choosing a male betta.

Try to pick out the healthiest looking betta that you possibly can because this will be the most attractive mate for a female.

Step #4: Let the Bettas Settle In

Once you've picked out your bettas, you'll need to let them settle into their new environment. Ideally this settling in period needs to last for a month, but no less than 2 weeks as a bare minimum.

It's also important to note that you'll want to keep the two bettas separate during this time. You can house them in the same aquarium if you like, but make sure you use a solid divider that won't allow them to see each other.

Doing so might cause too much stress while they are still trying to settle in. During this time, the main thing that you'll want to do is keep an eye on the bettas.

Make sure they're eating regularly and not showing any signs of illness. The last thing you want to do is try to breed a sick betta.

Once this settling in period is over, you can then move onto the next step...

Step #5: Set Up the Breeding Tank

Once both of your bettas have settled into their new environments, you'll want to set up your breeding tank. Here are the things you'll need to do to set up your breeding tank:

- Fill up the tank with 3-5 inches of water. The reason why you'll want to do this is that newborn fry will have a difficult time reaching the surface of the water to breathe and feed if the water is too deep.

- Get an almond leaf or use the bottom half of a Styrofoam cup for the male betta to be able to build his bubble nest.

- A heater to create the optimal temperature of 78-80 degrees Fahrenheit.

- Plants, moss, and other decorations. You'll want to add lots of plants and moss to your tank to give your fish plenty of different places to hide. Of course, you'll want to make sure that you don't overdo it to the point where your male and female can't find each other.

- Leave out the filter. Bettas prefer the water to be still when breeding, and any flow can disrupt the breeding process.

- Use an air pump. While you shouldn't use a filter because it could create too much flow, you should still use an air pump. This will help give the tank extra oxygen for the fry.

- Similarly to your regular betta tank set up, you'll want to let your breeding tank sit for 24 hours before you move your bettas into the tank to breed. This'll allow temperatures to stabilize and prevent your bettas from going into shock or not breeding because the water is too cold.

- Finally, you'll want to get a clear divider for the breeding tank. You might be tempted to immediately put the breeding pair in the tank together, but this would be a mistake. You need to give the male a chance to court and win over the female.

Step #6: Introducing the Breeding Pair

Like I just mentioned in the previous step, don't rush in and put both bettas in the breeding tank at the same time. Instead what you'll want to do is start by putting the female betta in on one side of the tank.

Leave her there (without the male on the other side) for approximately 30-45 minutes to let her get used to her new surroundings.

After this time period is up, you can then add the male betta to the other side. Once the bettas notice each other, the male betta should start doing things to try and attract the female such as flaring and turning a deeper color.

If your female is receptive to the male's advances, then you should notice vertical stripes along her midsection and a darkening in her colors.

If your female betta is bold she might even start to flirt back by flaring or wagging her body. If she's more on the shy side, she might clamp her fins to her body or even ignore the male.

These aren't necessarily signs that the female doesn't want to breed. If she still has the vertical stripes on her midsection, then you're still good to go so that's the main thing that you should be looking out for.

After this initial flirting period, you should start to notice the male betta building his bubble nest. His time will usually be divided between building the nest and coming back to the divider to show off to the female.

You'll want to make sure that you have the almond leaf or bottom half of the Styrofoam cup on the side of the male betta so he can build his bubble nest. Aside from that, you'll want to make sure that you leave the two bettas separated overnight.

You might be anxious to put them on the same side, but be patient you're almost there! The following day, you can go ahead and put your female in on the same side as your male.

After you place the female in on the other side, go ahead and put plastic wrap over the tank. This will help the tank to keep its humidity, which will aid in the hatching and development of the fry.

Once your male betta notices he can reach the female, his colors will become even more noticeable. He'll immediately start to try and chase the female around the tank to engage her in the mating dance.

During this time, you'll notice a lot of chasing and biting. Don't be alarmed, this is normal behavior during the mating process.

This is why you'll want to have plenty of plants, moss, and decorations in the tank in order to give the female plenty of places to hide if she gets tired. This part of chasing and biting can go on for hours.

If you don't notice the bettas engaging in the mating dance, then try dimming the lights in the room or adding more almond leaves to the tank to darken it. Bettas need their space and need to feel comfortable in order to mate.

This may not be necessary, but it's worth a try if your bettas aren't dancing. And if at any point you feel that the male is being too aggressive and is putting the female's safety in jeopardy, then remove her from that side of the tank.

Once your bettas decide to dance, you'll notice the male flip the female upside down and wrap himself around the female's midsection, and the couple will either float to the top or sink to the bottom of the tank.

After a few times of doing this, you'll notice the female starting to release eggs from her body. It might look as if the male is squeezing the eggs out of her body, but this is not what's going on.

The male is simply trying to increase the chance of fertilizing as many eggs as possible, hence why he's wrapped around the female the way that he is. Also, don't be alarmed if your female betta looks lifeless during parts of this process.

She may float on her side and appear dead, but she isn't— this is completely normal! Once eggs start falling out of her body, the male will start to pick them up and move them to the bubble nest.

And once your female has come out of her "lifeless" state, she may start to move eggs to the nest as well. However, you must pay attention here because she might try to eat the eggs.

Not only that, but after the mating process is complete, the male may see the female as a threat to the eggs and try to kill her. Therefore, it's best to not take any chances and remove the female from the breeding tank.

Once the eggs are in the nest, the male will look after the eggs for the next 1-2 days. The male will spend most of his time during this period attending to the eggs.

This might seem odd, but in the betta fish world, the male is the primary caregiver, not the female. By this point, the female is done with the process, and then male's role will be completed soon enough.

You may even notice the male eat some of the eggs; this of course, can be very upsetting but don't remove the male just yet.

He'll be needed for taking care of the fry when they initially hatch. Once the fry do start to hatch, some of them might fall from the bubble nest to the bottom of the tank.

If that happens, the male betta will pick up any fry that fall and put them back in the nest. He'll be very busy during this time making sure that all of the fry are ok, and this can be a lot of work depending on how many eggs there are!

During the first couple of days of life, the fry will be in a vertical position with their tail hanging down. After a few days, their bodies will start to move into a horizontal position and be able to swim freely.

Once the fry can move freely, go ahead and remove the adult male betta from the tank. Sometimes the male betta will eat the fry, and it's not worth the risk so simply remove him from the tank.

In terms of what you should feed the fry, you need to feed them live food. Feeding the fry the regular food you feed your adults such as pellets won't work.

This would include things such as small brine shrimp, vinegar eels, banana worms, or microworms. The good news is that fry grow fairly quickly.

At about one month of age, you'll already start to notice some visible and distinct colors in your bettas. And at 3-4 weeks you can go ahead and start feeding the fry finely grated frozen foods in addition to the live food.

Before 3-4 weeks of age, you'll want to stick strictly to the live food. It won't be until around 8-9 weeks of age that you can feed the bettas dry food such as pellets.

Yes, this might seem like quite a long period of time, but remember breeding bettas is time-consuming and expensive so make sure you know what you're getting yourself into before trying to breed bettas.

Aside from that, that's really all there is to breeding bettas. You must be patient though because it won't always work out perfectly with the bettas that you're trying to breed!

Chapter 8: Frequently Asked Questions

Can I place two males in the same tank together?

No, you should never place two male bettas in the same tank together. They're called Siamese Fighting Fish for a reason. In the wild, two male bettas will only span for a few minutes before one of them starts to flee.

However, in captivity there is no escape, and often times bettas will fight to the death. You might think that it would be fun to watch these fish fight, but there's nothing fun or entertaining about watching two fish try to kill each other.

Even if you only leave the fish together for a few minutes, they could seriously damage each other's fins and overall health. Please be wise and have the betta's best interest at heart. Don't put an animal through pain and suffering for your own enjoyment.

Can I place females in the same tank together?

You might be able to create what's known as a betta sorority tank. For this to work, the conditions must be right, and even then it doesn't work out sometimes. The first thing you'll need to get is a 10-gallon tank at a minimum, but 20 gallons would be even better.

The next thing you'll want to do is heavily decorate the tank with plants and other decorations. The size of the tank and the decorations will give the bettas plenty of space and allow them to get away and hide if need be. Aside from that, set up the tank the way you normally would with a single betta.

Finally, you'll want to make sure that you get at least 3 female bettas for the tank. If you only get two females, then one might dominate the other and bully it. Ideally though, you'd need to get 5-7 females, and if you decide to get more than 5, then you'll need to get a 20-gallon tank.

Once you have everything set up in the tank, keep a close eye on the fish. See how they are interacting with each other. If you notice a lot of fighting going on, then you'll need to separate the fish and place them in separate tanks. This is why it's important to have a backup plan in regards to what you'll do with the fish just in case the sorority tank doesn't work out.

Can I Put my Betta in a Tank with Other Fish?

Yes generally speaking you can put your betta fish in another tank that contains other tropical fish. The other fish in the tank need to be community fish—fish that get along with any species of fish. If you put semi-aggressive or aggressive fish in the tank with the betta, then the betta might get attacked.

Of course, you'll want to keep a close eye on your fish tank and see how the betta interacts with your other fish. Usually, it won't be a problem and the betta will get along with everyone else just fine. However, if you notice the betta getting aggressive or other fish getting aggressive towards you're betta, you'll need to have a backup plan for where to put your betta fish.

Should I Buy Water Specifically for Bettas?

At some pet stores, you might notice that they sell specific "betta water." This is supposed to be water that's made specifically for bettas. It's usually the size of a regular plastic bottle of water, but it costs around $4 per bottle!

That's seriously so insane and such a rip-off! This special "betta water" is simply conditioned water. Imagine how much money it would cost you to fill up your tank with this stuff, and then how much more you'd have to continue buying in order to do water changes.

It's absolutely absurd! You're much better off buying spring water by the gallon or getting a water conditioner at the pet store. Don't buy into the hype of the so-called "betta water," there's nothing special about it!

What Does it Mean When My Betta Builds a Bubble Nest?

A male betta building a bubble nest is simply a sign that your male is ready to mate. The breeding process will typically occur once the male builds a nest and then places the eggs released from the female into the nest and wait for them to hatch.

Of course, this doesn't mean that you have to find a female for your male to breed with or else he won't be happy. Building a bubble nest is simply a natural instinct for your betta, and it's a sign that he's happy and healthy—no need to breed if you don't want to! And also you don't have to worry if your betta isn't building a bubble nest, this doesn't necessarily mean that your betta isn't happy!

Why Does my Betta Fish Lay on the Bottom of the Tank?

You might be worried if you notice your betta lying at the bottom of the tank for long periods of time. Fear not because this is normal behavior.

If all others signs show that your betta is healthy, then there's nothing to worry about and your fish is simply lazing around. Bettas naturally like to sit on leaves or plants in the tank, and if you notice your betta lying in an unnatural position, then get some different plants or decorations for him to rest on or hide in.

Is my Betta Fish Going to Be Lonely By Himself?

The answer to that is no, your betta will be just fine by himself. If you want to put him in a community tank with other fish because you think that'd be more fun, then by all means do so. However, you don't have to worry about your fish getting bored or lonely by himself.

Bettas do just fine by themselves and many times are better off that way. There are certain kinds of fish that are known as schooling fish—such as a neon tetra. These fish don't like being alone and need to be with others of their kind or else they'll get stressed.

Bettas aren't like that at all—in fact, the males will fight if you put them together! Therefore, it's perfectly acceptable to have your betta in a tank by himself, but you can also put him in a community tank if you want to.

How Big Will My Betta Fish Get?

The typical size for an adult betta fish is 2.25 inches. However, in some instances, bettas will grow up to 3 inches in size if certain conditions are met like having a larger tank.

Why is my Betta Swimming Up and Down the Sides of the Tank?

If you notice your betta frequently swimming up and down the sides of your tank, take it as a sign that your betta probably isn't happy about something. This is known as glass surfing and it usually happens when your betta is stressed about something.

Usually, it'll occur when your tank has poor water conditions so make sure that you're doing regular water changes or invest in a filter. Your betta might also be glass surfing because the size of the tank is too small. Remember you'll want to get at least a tank size of 2.5 gallons for your betta fish.

Can my Betta Get Along with Other Tank Mates that Aren't Fish?

Yes, you can certainly test out other tank mates in your aquarium with your betta that aren't fish. The best options are mystery snails, ghost shrimp, and African dwarf frogs.

The cool thing about the snails and ghost shrimp is that they'll help to clean the tank while not creating too much waste themselves. Of course, you'll want to make sure you have a backup plan just in case your betta gets too aggressive with its new tank mates.

Conclusion

You now know everything you need in order to get started with taking care of a betta as a pet. Armed with this knowledge, you'll easily be able to give your betta the long and fulfilling life that it deserves. Sadly most people will never know this information, and they'll never learn how to properly take care of their betta fish. Luckily that isn't a problem for you anymore. Taking care of a betta fish is certainly fun, exciting, and well worth it! Thanks for reading!

60080129R00031